TAKE BACK YOUR LIFE

THE POWER PRAYER TO BANISH SATAN

CELESTE BROWN

© *Copyright 2019 - All rights reserved.*
Legal Notice: This book is copyright protected.
This book is only for personal use.

Contents

You CAN Be Free _____ 1

Why You Are Under Attack _____ 4

My Story _____ 7

What Scripture Has To Say _____ 15

Before Reading The Prayer _____ 21

The Prayer _____ 22

Afterthoughts On The Prayer ____ 26

How To Use It To Best Effect _____ 29

Keep Up The Good Fight:
Why Persistence Pays _____ 33

Now It's Your Duty To Help Others __ 37

You CAN Be Free

Demonic possession, war with Satan, malevolent entities — terms such as these might sound plain crazy to you. You could be forgiven for assuming they belong to fringe religious movements that have very little to do with everyday Christianity and living in the Word. If this is the case for you, I don't blame you one bit — this is exactly how I used to feel.

On the other hand, maybe you've had first-hand experience with dark forces or know someone who has suffered as a result of their influence. In that case you might be more open to accepting that evil forces can wreak havoc with people's lives and that they undoubtedly exist in a realm we know little about.

In either case, I can attest to you in good Christian faith and from personal experience that malevolent forces DO indeed exist and there is a good chance that they are influencing your life to a greater or lesser degree.

Sometimes its small, such as you always seem to have bad luck and few things ever seem to go right for you. In more serious cases — when you are targeted by a powerful malign entity — it can turn your life upside down. It can ruin your health, your relationships, your finances, and then spread out to your family.

The ultimate enemy — Satan — has one goal. To lay waste to your life and take your attention off the Word. This usually starts in small ways but over time — like an open wound that festers and then becomes infected — it will escalate until eventually you end up in a very dark place where you feel all hope is lost. Make no mistake, Satan wants you weak, vulnerable and without hope — because then he can influence you to do his bidding without resistance.

However, I want to make one thing crystal clear — there IS a way to remove him and his dark influence from your life for good. In this book I will share with you the special prayer that has cast out all evil forces from my own life. Since learning of this prayer, I have used it to help many other people remove evil from their life and regain the vitality, good fortune and abundance they deserve.

This is not a long book, as I don't believe in writing endless theory, filler and fluff just to fill out more pages. That would be a disservice to you and a waste of your time. My goal is to give you the essential facts and knowledge NOW — so you can start taking action TODAY.

So let's begin learning how to take back your life.

Celeste Brown

Why You Are Under Attack

Before we move on there is one thing I need to address. It's a question that I have been asked so many times in my spiritual work and also the question I kept on asking during my long period of darkness. That question is: why me? Why have I been targeted for spiritual attack by malevolent forces? Is it because I am a bad person? Is it because I have offended the Lord in some manner and have been forsaken? Is it because someone has wished misfortune and ruin on me?

Firstly, I would like you to know that I have helped teachers, medics, volunteers and pastors. Some of the nicest and most giving people you could ever meet. You are NOT in this situation because you are a bad person or you have taken some action that has inadvertently summoned evil entities. It is also not because someone has wished you harm. Those who attempt to use dark means to harm others always — sooner or later — see this backfire on them spectacularly.

The fact is that at some point you were finding life hard and your faith was shaken — this happens to everyone. A dark force used this opportunity to grasp the smallest toehold into your life and, over time, this malign influence has grown in the shadows. Think of it as a flu virus or a parasite. When your immune system is strong you have stern defenses to ensure no external contamination can enter your body and do you harm. However, when your immune system is weakened then your body does not have the strength to shield you from outside threats. This is when you become infected and then sick. You are dealing with a spiritual sickness in your life.

Think back upon your life now and when you first suspected that an external force could be the cause of your problems. When did this suspicion first arise? Now cast your mind back even further to before that point. Did you suffer some kind of misfortune, injury or loss, and did this, even just temporarily, shake your faith? In my healing work with dozens upon dozens of people, the answer is invariably yes.

Your defenses were down and something sinister saw the opportunity to attach itself to you. Like a cancer, it has grown over time. Like a cancer, its ultimate aim is to take you over completely. Like a cancer, it will not go into remission and die without drastic intervention.

The good news is that the healing teaching inside this book is the spiritual equivalent of the most powerful cancer drug ever created. It has the power to obliterate the cancerous entities that have been plaguing you and ensure that they never return — ever. What's more, it has the power to protect your loved ones. These evil forces will have no path to infect (or re-infect) your family and home. We will deal with this once and for all.

My Story

My name is Celeste Brown and I am a wife and mother of three from Wisconsin in the US.

The truth is, there is nothing special about me. I was never visited by angels as a child, I was never particularly studious in Bible study while growing up, and I don't claim to have the power to lay my hands on you and cure you of your afflictions. But what I can say, however, is that I am living proof that you can banish the forces of darkness from your existence and reclaim your life so it can once again be glorious and fulfilling. This is my own personal miracle.

I did not achieve this by having any special powers, but by a 'chance encounter' with a man who changed my life. Of course, I now know that these things do not happen by chance and that there was a purpose behind this event. That purpose was to use my experience of salvation to spread the knowledge I attained, so others too can reclaim their lives. This is the reason why I have written this book and, by God's grace, have been able to deliver its knowledge to readers such as yourself.

Now let's take a brief overview of my story.

Ten years ago I found myself on the brink of divorce, my health was deteriorating fast, my children were failing at school and I was in a constant state of mental distress.

Things started to go wrong in my life slowly at first. After a very normal life up until my mid-30s, I suddenly became very prone to injuries, car accidents and coming down with lots of minor illnesses such as the flu and chest infections. I thought it was just a run of bad luck but, after a while of continual misfortune, I started questioning if other people have this much bad luck in their lives. From what I could see, I doubted it.

One day I slipped on the pavement and landed very awkwardly, breaking the metatarsal bone in my left foot. Not only was this agonizingly painful, but it meant I had to be off work for an extended period. I was still in the probationary period of my new job so my employer used my injury as an excuse to let me go.

The restriction on my movement didn't allow me to do much around the house, which meant my husband was required to step up to ensure our kids were taken care of and the house was maintained in some kind of order. In the past, he was always only too happy to help out around the house, but suddenly he deeply resented the extra burden placed on him. He was sullen, snappy and seemed to have a lot of anger directed at me.

At the same time, my two sons (twins), and their younger sister began facing a number of challenges. The boys became disruptive in school and we were told that they would face suspension if their behavior didn't improve. My daughter became withdrawn, had sleeping difficulties and was very quick to anger. All this was unlike any of my three children who, up until that point, were cheerful, studious and generally well-behaved.

I was then struck down by the worst chest infection of my life, which landed me in hospital on a drip, feeling as if I had an elephant sitting on my chest. That night on the hospital ward I took stock of my life. It was unfathomable to me why my family were acting so out of character and why I was facing health challenge after health challenge. Yes, my foot injury had disrupted our home life, but it didn't explain why those closest to me were now seemingly different people to those I knew and loved.

At this time words such as Satan, spirits and demonic forces did not even enter my mind.

The strong steroids prescribed to me finally calmed my chest enough for me to leave hospital and, using crutches, I was able to hobble around my local area.

On one of my walks I visited a bookstore and was immediately drawn to the small section on Christianity. As I leafed through the various books, I felt a tap on my shoulder. I turned to find a very old man with a cane in one hand and a well-thumbed Bible in the other. Despite his advanced age, he had radiant blue eyes which signaled both his benevolence and sharpness of mind.

He introduced himself only as Father Ryan, a retired pastor, and asked what I was looking for. As he stared at me with those perceptive eyes, I began crying. I didn't have any explanation for this and it was out of character for me, to say the least. He put down his Bible, took my hand and simply said "Let it out". Not only did I let out my tears but I also let out my story of what had become of my life and my family. I confessed that I had no explanation for what had befallen us and I was in desperate need.

He listened carefully and intently and offered his sympathies, but then said something that took me aback. He asked me if I had considered the influence of Satan. He went on to explain that he'd had a long career in ministry and clusters of bad occurrences, such as I was experiencing, often pointed to the work of demonic forces. I was far from convinced.

He offered me a prayer that he claimed he had used successfully to defeat dark forces throughout his career. I was skeptical but I didn't want to offend this kind man who had taken the time to listen to my troubles. So I borrowed a pen and scrap of paper from the cashier and wrote down the prayer, which he recited to me from memory. It is the exact same prayer you will find later in this book.

I must admit that I only wrote down the prayer because I didn't want to offend Father Ryan, rather than to actually use it. I was a firm non-believer in all things dark and demonic. To me, it was all just woo-woo nonsense.

However, he once more took my hand and asked me to promise him that I would at least try the prayer. So, in Christian fellowship, I agreed and took note of his instructions on how to use it to best effect.

So now I was obliged to at least try the prayer. A part of me was annoyed that I had been made to do something that I didn't think could work. Another part of me was open to the possibility that there could be some truth to the prayer, which I had to admit as I wrote it down, was very powerful. The fact I had few other options or ideas was no doubt another reason why I at least gave it a try. So I began in earnest that very day.

About a week after using this prayer, I remember it was a Wednesday afternoon and I was in my garden, I felt a huge weight lifted off my chest. This was not simply the chest infection finally leaving my body. I can only describe it as a mental fog, cloud of pessimism and dark energy evaporating. The funny thing was it was only after these things were gone that I realized they were there in the first place. These feelings had become such an ingrained part of my being that I thought they were a just a part of my nature. Only after I tasted this sweet freedom — even as it began to rain in my garden — did I know beyond doubt that I had been in the grip of dark forces. No other power could have laid waste to my life and household so thoroughly for all these years. I fell to my knees to give thanks.

I knew I was free at last. I also knew with every fiber of my being that this prayer would serve as my spiritual armor. It would never allow dark forces to enter my life or home again. I now had a powerful weapon against Satan and, like the coward he is, he went off looking for easier defenseless prey. That's how he works, he will always go for the low-hanging fruit, the easy option. That was not me, not anymore.

In time, I was able to save my marriage and show my children a more productive path for their lives. It transpired that my daughter's behavior was due to her being introduced to a powerful variety of the drug marijuana. She was able to kick the habit and swore on the Holy Book that she had forsaken it forever.

I won't pretend to you that our lives transformed over night. It took work and it took counseling. However, I clearly sensed that the forces that kept us in bondage to mistrust, negativity and misfortune had lifted. We finally had the chance to heal and shine light into the areas where there was only darkness before.

Seeing the changes in those you love is truly the greatest blessing.

What Scripture Has To Say

So far I have talked about my opinion and experiences. Now it's time to back this up with scripture.

Whenever someone is trying to convince you of anything, always look to the Good Book for confirmation that you are being led down the correct path. This is particularly the case when dealing with spiritual matters. Never take a course of action without their being precedent in the Bible.

In this chapter we will look at some key passages of scripture that shed light on the fight we have before us and the tools we need to defeat Satan and his minions.

Let's start with the Bible's description of the nature of spiritual warfare with the forces of evil.

Ephesians 6:11-13

"Put on the full armor of God, so that you will be able to stand firm against the schemes of the devil. For our struggle is not against flesh and blood, but against the rulers, against the powers, against the world forces of this darkness, against the spiritual forces of wickedness in the heavenly places. Therefore, take up the full armor of God, so that you will be able to resist in the evil day, and having done everything, to stand firm."

Peter 5:8

"Be sober-minded; be watchful. Your adversary the devil prowls around like a roaring lion, seeking someone to devour."

> *2 Corinthians 10:3–5*
>
> *"For though we walk in the flesh, we are not waging war according to the flesh. For the weapons of our warfare are not of the flesh but have divine power to destroy strongholds. We destroy arguments and every lofty opinion raised against the knowledge of God, and take every thought captive to obey Christ."*

These passages describe wonderfully the nature of the battle we are facing. We are dealing with a cunning, deceptive and fierce enemy that "prowls around ... seeking someone to devour". This is Satan looking for his next victim.

We are also told "we are not waging war according to the flesh" and that "our struggle" is against the "spiritual forces of wickedness". This shows that we are not fighting a conventional battle and we need to combat Satan's influence in the spiritual, rather than physical, realm if he is to be defeated.

We are also told to "Put on the full armor of God, so that you will be able to stand firm against the schemes of the devil". Remember, we are talking about spiritual armor, which is prayer, belief and conviction.

Now let's look at a few passages about how we might find salvation.

Colossians 1:13

"He has delivered us from the domain of darkness and transferred us to the kingdom of his beloved Son"

Timothy 2:25-26

"Correcting his opponents with gentleness. God may perhaps grant them repentance leading to a

> *knowledge of the truth, and they may come to their senses and escape from the snare of the devil, after being captured by him to do his will."*

Matthew 4:10

> *"Then Jesus said to him, "Be gone, Satan! For it is written, 'You shall worship the Lord your God and him only shall you serve.'"*

I hope that these three passages bring courage and bravery to your heart. They teach us that, when it comes to battle, Satan is no match for God. "He has delivered us from the domain of darkness" is a line that we must keep particularly close to hearts. For it is the very outcome we are seeking. We now know that we CAN escape the domain of darkness and "the snare of the devil". Be bold. Be brave. We are arming ourselves with spiritual weaponry to defeat demonic influence.

I want to highlight one more line of scripture before we move on.

James 4:7

"Submit yourselves, then, to God. Resist the devil, and he will flee from you."

This sentence goes to the absolute heart of this book and the prayer contained within it. You need to submit yourself to God and ask for his only son's strength in helping you come back into the light. Put aside pride and submit to the only higher power that can save you and your family. Come to this teaching with humility and obedience and let it work miracles for you.

Before Reading The Prayer

The prayer is contained in the next chapter. Before reading it I would like to ask you to just prepare a little.

Please find a quiet place where you will not be disturbed so you can read the prayer in peace and serenity. If you are surrounded by hustle and bustle at this present time, why not read it later when you have more calm and mental space.

After you have read the prayer, I would ask you to take a few minutes just to do nothing and sit in stillness. Allow a little time to contemplate what you have just read.

Allow any feelings to surface and be in the moment with the prayer and the words. Notice your emotions and any sensations that arise within you. Then move on to the next chapter entitled 'Afterthoughts On The Prayer'.

The Prayer

Jesus, I can sense the ominous presence of darkness around me.

I recognize my enemy is at work to discourage me, to lead me into temptation, to take my eyes away from you. I feel helpless in this storm, O' Lord.

I need your supernatural power to stand strong and not surrender. My bodily force will not help because, as you have decreed, the weapons of warfare are different from those in the material world.

As believers, our weapons are powerful and can demolish dark strongholds and lies. These supernatural weapons originate from you, and you alone, Lord.

By your precious name in blood, Jesus, I am asking you to confound Satan and end his attempt to lay waste to my life and do harm unto my kin.

Help me not to become discouraged or to succumb when the times of testing come. When I am tired and weak, you are strong, Lord, and you are my only source of salvation. I cannot fight without you.

I trust you to pull down these strongholds that keep me and my family helpless. Guard us from isolation that leaves us exposed and vulnerable.

You destroyed the power of my enemy by your death and resurrection. But the fight is not done. My enemy keeps whispering lies, twisting truths and attempting to inflate my selfish pride.

I am declaring the Devil and his demons liars today, O' Lord. Through the power of your precious name and blood, I agree with your Word and the truth that you are in me and that you are greater than my enemies who plot to replace you.

You, your Word, and prayer are my secret weapons. I belong to you, and that fills me with the power and purpose to reclaim my life. I want to be clothed constantly in the spiritual armor that you offer me. Help me use it to defend myself and others from Satan's fiery darts.

Strengthen my faith, Lord. Forgive my sins so that I may be clean in your righteousness. Make me brave so I can stand and fight the spiritual battle for my life. Give me your wisdom and discernment so I will not be caught off-guard.

Together, Lord, we WILL conquer darkness because, in truth, you already have.

In Jesus' powerful name, before which ALL shall bow. Amen.

Afterthoughts On The Prayer

I hope you've had a chance to reflect on the prayer. If not, please take a moment now.

How did it make you feel when you read it?

Did it accurately convey your feelings about your situation?

Did it give you a sense of hope?

Do you feel it will arm you with a sharp tool to defeat the darkness in your life?

If you are anything like me, then you had an emotional reaction as you read the words and contemplated the prayer. A sense of hope rose up inside of you – a spark that will turn into a flame and devour your enemy.

Let's look at why the prayer is so powerful.

It admits you need help

As mentioned in the chapter on scripture, now is the time to put aside pride and submit. The prayer admits that we are helpless in the face of this onslaught and we need both spiritual defenses and spiritual weapons to fight. This we ask for from Christ with humility.

It calls out the Devil

The prayer exposes Satan as a liar and manipulator. This is important as it shows we are no longer a part of his devious scheme. We are not blindly following his will and allowing our lives to spiral downwards. We have grown wise to his presence and we are calling him out of the shadows. Once he is exposed, he can be attacked.

It places Jesus above all dark entities

The prayer states unambiguously that ALL must bow before Jesus. In asking for help from the Savior, we reaffirm that no Satanic force can stand before the light of Christ. He is the King of

Kings and we state loud and clear that his strength cannot be matched by any demonic force.

<u>The battle has been won before</u>

There is a very important line towards the end of the prayer — 'we WILL conquer darkness because, in truth, you already have'. This attests to the fact that Jesus has already defeated Satan by never once giving in to his temptations. So we are affirming that it has been PROVEN that Satan is no match for Jesus. Hence, we are asking for the aid of an unbeaten ally.

How To Use It To Best Effect

So now we know the prayer and have looked at why it is so effective. Next we must learn how to use it to best effect. The two important questions are: How often do we pray, and at what time?

Father Ryan gave me the answer to this question when he offered me the prayer. However, before I share his answer with you, I feel it is wise to examine the Bible to fully understand the evidence for this instruction.

Deuteronomy 6: 4-9

"Love the LORD your God with all your heart and with all your soul and with all your strength. These commandments that I give you today are to be upon your hearts. Impress them on your children. Talk about them when you sit at home and when you walk along the road,

> *when you lie down and when you get up. Tie them as symbols on your hands and bind them on your foreheads"*

Notice the instruction to talk about the commands of God "when you lie down and when you get up". Devout Christians understood this to mean to meditate on the Bible at the beginning of the day and at the end of the day.

The Old Testament book, Joshua, confirms the importance of meditating twice a day on the Scriptures.

> *Chapter 1, verse 8.*

> *"Do not let this Book of the Law depart from your mouth; meditate on it day and night, so that you may be careful to do everything written in it. Then you will be prosperous and successful."*

Jesus himself emphasized the need to persevere with prayer. He indicated that Christians must pray at least two times per day — during the day and at night.

> Luke 18, verse 1
>
> *"And will not God bring about justice for his chosen ones, who cry out to him day and night? Will he keep putting them off? I tell you, he will see that they get justice, and quickly. However, when the Son of Man comes, will he find faith on the earth?"*

This verse shows God's desire that his followers would cry out to Him "day and night". However, the question that the parable concludes on, is the question of whether faith exists among God's people. Do his chosen ones have the faith to believe Him that their prayers are effectual? In this passage, Jesus plainly states his desire that Christians should pray every day and every night.

So, in answer to the two questions I posed at the beginning of this chapter: in the morning after you wake up and in the evening before you retire to sleep are the times when this prayer is the most effective. Do this every day without fail until you are victorious in your battle. Do not waver in your commitment or conviction.

Keep Up The Good Fight: Why Persistence Pays

I ended the previous chapter with a call for you to be committed to this process and steadfast in your prayers. Let's look at why this is so crucial in securing victory over demonic forces and freeing your life.

When you start your prayer practice there will be times when you will doubt whether this can truly work for you. You may question whether a prayer you read in a short book really has the ability to dramatically alter the course of your life.

You may even question whether the misfortunes you have experienced are actually down to the influence of dark forces. Maybe you were mistaken — isn't that Devil stuff all superstitious mumbo-jumbo?

When these thoughts enter your mind — and it is likely they will — ask yourself this. Where do these thoughts come from? More importantly, ask yourself, WHO do these thoughts come from?

Who wants you to lose faith in your actions? Who wants you to stop this day and night praying? Who wants you to end your call to the King of Kings to dress you in spiritual armor? Who wants you right back where you were before? Who wants you docile and susceptible to their plans? Who is whispering to you from the shadows?

I think you need no answer from me.

I do not know you. I do not know whether you are young or old, I do not know if you are male or female. But I know that you will be tempted to stray from the right path — just as Satan tempted Jesus while he fasted for 40 days and nights in the Judean Desert.

What did Jesus do? Did he just give in?

No! He remained steadfast and resisted each and every temptation. It was only after this spiritual trial that he returned to Galilee to begin his ministry. And it is only after this trial of temptation that you will be free of malign influences. This is YOUR test. Remain committed and submit to Christ. Persistence is your path to victory.

Now let's look at an excellent example from the mouth of Jesus himself.

Luke 11:5-13

Jesus said to His disciples, "Which of you shall have a friend, and go to him at midnight and say to him, 'Friend, lend me three loaves; for a friend of mine has come to me on his journey, and I have nothing to set before him'; and he will answer from within and say, 'Do not trouble me; the door is now shut, and my children are with me in bed; I cannot rise and give to you'? I say to you, though he will not rise and give to him because he is his friend, yet because of his

> *persistence, he will rise and give him as many as he needs."*

I'll help to explain this parable. A man has a friend come to visit him. But the man has no bread to offer. So he goes to his next-door neighbor and says: "Lend me three loaves of bread". The neighbor replies: "I can't do it. I'm already in bed. Don't bother me".

Jesus then explains: "I say to you, though he will not rise and give to him because he is his friend, yet because of his persistence, he will rise and give him as many as he needs."

I want to repeat the final part one more time: "yet because of his persistence, he will rise and give him as many as he needs".

Jesus is teaching us that persistence will get you what you need — there will be no limit to what you will receive.

Please take this to heart.

Now It's Your Duty To Help Others

If you are steadfast in your prayers and have the persistence to ignore all distractions then, like me, you will be free of demonic influences.

You will know when this happens. It will be an unmistakable sensation in body, mind and soul. You will experience the sudden lifting of a heaviness that has been weighing you down for so long.

I have every faith that this will come to pass for you. When it does however, your work is not done.

I believe that it is our solemn duty to help others once we have experienced the joy of healing. When you have expelled Satan, what is he going to do?

Remember the words of Peter 5:8

> *"Your adversary the devil prowls around like a roaring lion, seeking someone to devour."*

That's right. Once you have cast him out and erected strong spiritual defenses that he cannot penetrate, he will slink away and look for an easy target. Someone who is down on their luck and maybe undergoing a momentary crisis of faith.

It is not Christian to ignore the plight of our brothers and sisters. Just because we are personally free of dark influences, the war against darkness is not won. It is still our collective duty to fight the good fight on behalf of humanity.

How can you do this?

Share your example, give away this book to those in need, make copies of the prayer to distribute to your congregation. Use social media or word of mouth. Become a beacon of hope for those who are wrestling with evil.

I will leave you with the Bible verse that I have taken to heart since being healed. I hope it inspires you too.

Hebrews 6:10

"God is not unjust; he will not forget your work and the love you have shown him as you have helped his people and continue to help them."

Wishing you nothing but love and light.
Celeste Brown

www.ingramcontent.com/pod-product-compliance
Lightning Source LLC
Chambersburg PA
CBHW071039080526
44587CB00015B/2696